It dawns, and as the sun takes its place in the sky,
and clears the shadows of our memory, we remember
the stories our grandparents told us.

This is an Em Querido book
Published by Levine Querido

LQ
LEVINE QUERIDO

www.levinequerido.com • info@levinequerido.com

Levine Querido is distributed by Chronicle Books, LLC

Originally published in Mexico by Fondo de Cultura Ecónomica

Library of Congress Control Number: 2022945160
ISBN 978-1-64614-251-4

Printed and bound in China

Published in March 2023
Fourth Printing

The text type was set in Cochin.

David Álvarez created his illustrations with
acrylics and oil paints, later digitized.

Ancient Night

DAVID ÁLVAREZ

WITH DAVID BOWLES

LQ

LEVINE QUERIDO

MONTCLAIR • AMSTERDAM • HOBOKEN

*A*t the start of things, the elders say,
the universe was hushed and still.
The moon alone shone bright and round
in the star-speckled dark of the sky.

To keep its light forever a-glow,
Rabbit made her way down
the Great Ceiba's trunk
and trekked across
the sea-ringed world...

…to bring back more aguamiel,
the precious, glowing nectar
that brims in the heart
of the first and holy maguey.

Clever Opossum
had watched the moon
grow brighter
and dimmer
and brighter again
with every passing night.

He waited in hiding
till at last he caught sight
of Rabbit, his rival,
refilling the moon.

Why should you *get every drop?* he thought.

I want to taste the nectar, too.

Surprised the sky was dark,
Rabbit set out to follow
a bobbing circle of light.

She found Opossum
drinking deep
from his stolen jug
of sacred sap.

"Foolish Opossum,
what have you done?"
Rabbit cried out.
"Now, no heavenly light
can shine upon the earth!"

Full of regret and shame,
Opossum fled to his home underground.
Then, he recalled a treasure
hidden deep within the earth.

He went searching for that fire
prepared by mighty gods
as a gift for future humans
who might shiver in the dark.

To steal it cost the fur
from the tip of Opossum's tail,
but soon he set the blazing sun
high in its place in the sky.

Now, as the glow of the moon
fades with the dawning sun,
Opossum and Rabbit,
Guardians of Light,

sip their aguamiel together
sharing the stories that they hear
on their many epic treks
across the sea-ringed world.

A NOTE FROM THE CREATORS

Ancient Night presents a twist on several traditional stories of Mesoamerica—what we now call Mexico and Central America—weaving them into a tale that we hope feels both new and timeless. Here are some of the elements that we drew together:

THE GREAT CEIBA

In most Mesoamerican creation stories, especially among Maya and Nahua people, the heavens are held up by the branches of a massive tree, usually a ceiba. This "World Tree" is thought of as the tail of a huge caiman or alligator, whose knobby skin is a lot like the spiny trunk of a ceiba. Many Maya groups believe the Great Ceiba to be an entire ancient caiman. Most Nahuas consider it to be just the tail, while the Earth itself was made by the gods from the body of the ancient caiman that they call Cipactli.

In any case, the roots of the tree are where the Underworld sits. For people in Mesoamerica, this wasn't just a place where people's spirits went. The moon and sun also spent half the day in the Underworld, resting and getting their light replenished by the god of fire.

RABBIT AND THE MOON

For people in Mesoamerica, the dark spots on the moon are the tracks of a rabbit. There are different versions of why a rabbit went to the moon. Some stories claim the moon once shone as bright as the sun—even though the god who became the moon had been afraid to step into the divine bonfire, while the god who became the sun had bravely entered the flames. To remind the world that the moon was not as heroic as the sun, a rabbit was hurled to the moon to stamp on his face and lessen his glow.

Other tales see the rabbit as a caretaker of the moon, lifted there as a gift by gods who recognized her selfless goodness. In some Maya traditions, the rabbit is the oldest son of the moon, who runs away until caught by the sun and returned to his mother.

OPOSSUM AND THE SUN'S FIRE

Another animal figure revered throughout Mesoamerica is the opossum. Mazatec traditions say he ruled the world in a time before humans lived in cities. The Cora people name him Yaushu.

This opossum was both silly and wise, best known for loving people enough to take great risks for them. In one story, for example, humans let their fire go out. It was created by lightning, so they have no way to restart it. They beg Yaushu to help them, so he follows the sun as it sets, into the Underworld, carrying pots of pulque with him. He shares the drink with the God of Fire, who has just stoked the flames of the sun. The god has so much pulque, he falls asleep. Yaushu finally has his chance to steal fire from the divine hearth, but there's no wood left to make a torch!

Instead, the opossum sets his tail aflame and runs quickly back to the world of the living. His humans are waiting with a huge pile of kindling, and Yaushu restarts their bonfire. Now the tails of opossums are forever bald.

MAGUEY AND AGUAMIEL

The opossum is also famous for discovering aguamiel, the delicious sap of the maguey that grows all over Mesoamerica. With his nimble, almost human hands, he could dig into the heart of the plant to get at the honeyed liquid, which became a boon to those who live in the desert. Aguamiel calms thirst, provides energy, contains protein, and has medicinal properties.

Eventually, according to some tales, the opossum learned to let aguamiel sit and ferment into a strong wine called pulque. But the Tlapanec people say the opossum stole pulque from the gods, to give to humanity so that they could be warm even without fire. The only problem was that opossum was the biggest drinker of all! One day he had so much pulque, he stumbled all over Mesoamerica, his tail zigzagging along the ground and creating the snaking curves that would become our rivers.

WEAVING STORIES

For thousands of years, the peoples of Mesoamerica have retold these stories and many, many more, changing them bit by bit, adding and subtracting the ideas that matter to them. Even today, you can hear new versions in communities across Mexico and Central America. In this book, we have done the same: pairing up the rabbit and the opossum made creative sense to us. They are both associated with major lights in our skies, and tying them together along with the Great Ceiba and aguamiel felt like imagining a much older version of their tales, something truly ancient, from a time long forgotten, when wise and foolish animals ruled the world, waiting for humans to finally emerge.